O N E N E S S

ONENESS

GREAT PRINCIPLES
SHARED BY ALL RELIGIONS

JEFFREY MOSES

*With an Introduction
and Special Prayer from*

MOTHER TERESA

FAWCETT COLUMBINE • NEW YORK

To Ruth, whose love and devotion
helped bring this book to light.

With special thanks to Dr. Anita Figuerado,
who introduced me to Mother Teresa.

A Fawcett Columbine Book
Published by Ballantine Books
Copyright © 1989 by Jeffrey Moses

Library of Congress Cataloging-in-Publication Data
Moses, Jeffrey.
Oneness : great principles shared by all religions / Jeffrey Moses
; with an introduction and a special prayer from Mother Teresa.
p.   cm.
Bibliography: p.
ISBN 0-449-90437-7
1. Religions—Relations.   I. Title.
BL410.M67   1989
291—dc20   88-92870
CIP

Design by Holly Johnson
Manufactured in the United States of America

First Edition: November 1989
10 9 8 7 6 5 4 3 2 1

*"I pray that this book accomplishes
what God wants it to."*

MOTHER TERESA

CONTENTS

Foreword   1

The Golden Rule   3

Honor Thy Father and Mother   7

There Is One God   11

Speak Truth   15

More Blessed to Give Than to Receive   19

Heaven Is Within   23

Love Thy Neighbor   27

Conquer with Love   31

Blessed Are the Peacemakers   35

As Ye Sow, So Shall Ye Reap   39

A Man Is Known by His Deeds,
    Not by His Religion   43

Not Words or Detachment, but Action   47

Better to Examine the Self   51

Better to Rule the Spirit   55

Wisdom Is More than Riches   59

Man Does Not Live by Bread Alone   63

Do Not Harm Anything   67

Blessed to Forgive   71

Be Slow to Anger   75

Judge Not   79

Follow the Spirit of the Scriptures,
    Not the Letter   83

Start When Young to Seek Wisdom   87

Be Wholehearted   91
Honor the Elderly   95
Our True Strength   99
God Is Love   103
Man Is Created in God's Image   107
Living in Unity   111
Prayers of the Religions   115
Conclusion   118
Sources   119

FOREWORD

Throughout the ages, the scriptures of all religions have proclaimed that humanity is one great family. This is a simple truth, and it is simply and directly stated in every religion. In fact, almost all the principles that are associated with religious thought are shared by every religion. The Golden Rule, Love Thy Neighbor, Honor Thy Father and Mother, Speak Truth, It Is More Blessed to Give Than to Receive—these principles and others are common to all religions and are very similarly expressed in each.

This book discusses many of these fundamental precepts and shows their similarity of expression. Each page was put together with the awareness that modern words can hardly add to the immensity of the world's collected spiritual wisdom. For this reason the commentaries are short, allowing the sayings to speak for themselves.

The principles in this book form the basis for structuring an individual's life. The great sayings are like a guide or a blueprint for the inner development of mind and spirit that allows a person to achieve his highest goals. These principles are the foundation for success in personal relationships with family and friends, for satisfaction and success in business activities, and for that final aspiration in life that each person ultimately desires—the achievement of inner peace extending beyond the confines of an individual lifetime.

These great principles are not limiting to a person's satisfaction and fulfillment. Instead, they are guidelines that enable men and women to evolve to the highest point of human consciousness, wherein oneness is achieved with all the laws of nature. They allow men to avoid mistakes, to take the path of growth and achievement, and to answer the urgent and vital questions that ultimately arise.

Many people today seek their own laws. Yet in so doing, they often find only partial values of these universal principles. In actuality, the full values of these universal principles have been recorded similarly in all major religions since time immemorial. The principles of inner development are basically no different now than they were in the days of Jesus, Buddha, Mohammad, Shankara, or Confucious. These great masters offer similar messages that have not become less essential for people in the modern world. These principles stretch beyond time and change. They establish a clearly marked path which will enable each individual to attain the peace and enlightenment that is the ultimate goal in life.

I am sure that if we all understand The Golden Rule—that God is Love and that He has created us for greater things, to love and to be loved—we would then love one another as He has loved each one of us. True love is a giving until it hurts. It is not how much we give—but how much love we put into the giving.

Therefore it is necessary to pray—the fruit of prayer is deepening of Faith—the fruit of Faith is Love—Love in action is Service—and so acts of Love are acts of Peace—and this is the living of The Golden Rule.

Love one another as God loves each one of us.

God Bless You,
Mother Teresa

Do unto others as you would have them do unto you, for this is the law and the prophets.

Christianity

What is hurtful to yourself do not to your fellow man. That is the whole of the Torah and the remainder is but commentary.

Judaism

Do unto all men as you would wish to have done unto you; and reject for others what you would reject for yourselves.

Islam

Hurt not others with that which pains yourself.

Buddhism

Tzu-Kung asked: "Is there one principle upon which one's whole life may proceed?" The Master replied, "Is not Reciprocity such a principle?—what you do not yourself desire, do not put before others."

Confucianism

This is the sum of all true righteousness—
Treat others, as thou wouldst thyself be treated.
Do nothing to thy neighbor, which hereafter
Thou wouldst not have thy neighbor do to thee.

Hinduism

HONOR THY FATHER
AND MOTHER

It would be difficult to repay our parents for the hours, days, and years they cared for us when we were young. Perhaps the only way to return some of that love is through caring for our own children, and for our parents as they grow older.

We should do our best to know our parents, for knowing them is the key to knowing ourselves. The day will come when we shall wish we had known them better.

HONOR THY FATHER
AND MOTHER

My son, keep your father's commandment, and forsake not your mother's teaching. Bind them upon your heart always; tie them about your neck. When you walk, they will lead you; when you lie down, they will watch over you; and when you awake, they will talk with you.

Judaism

For God commanded, saying, Honor thy father and mother.

Christianity

Honor thy Father and Mother. Forget not the favours thou hast received.

Hinduism

Serve and revere your parents. Heaven is spread
beneath the feet of mothers everywhere.

Islam

To support Father and Mother,
To cherish Wife and Child,
To follow a peaceful calling,
This is the greatest blessing.

Buddhism

If each man would love his parents and show
due respect to his elders, the whole empire
would enjoy tranquillity.

Confucianism

THERE IS
ONE GOD

Nature, Being, the Absolute, or an actual name for God—whatever term man uses, his almost universal belief that there is one God shows a profound oneness of the human spirit.

Such a belief reveals a conviction that an ultimate existence pervades all the boundaries of the universe, and that all people and all things are of one essence.

THERE IS
ONE GOD

There is one God and Father of all, who is above
all, and through all, and in you all.

Christianity

Have we not all one Father? Has not one God
created us?

Judaism

He is the one God hidden in all beings, all-
pervading, the Self within all beings, watching
over all worlds, dwelling in all beings, the
witness, the perceiver.

Hinduism

Remember even when alone that the Divine is everywhere.

Confucianism

There is but one God whose name is true. He is the creator, immortal, unborn, self-existent.

Sikhism

SPEAK TRUTH

A man cannot be untruthful in one area of his life without having that influence permeate every other sphere. Untruthfulness creates habits in the personality that ultimately affect everything that a man wishes to accomplish. A man cannot speak lies while at work and then, later in the day, be entirely truthful with his family. Love and inner growth are enhanced by speaking truthfully. If only for personal fulfillment, a man should cultivate truthfulness in all aspects of his life.

On another level no less important, untruthfulness indicates an ignorance of the intrinsic oneness of all people. An individual will lie only when he thinks that he is separate from others and that he can make a significant advancement in life by impeding the progress of others. Any advantage gained by untruthfulness is temporary at best, because the most fundamental and important activity in life—the development of an awareness of God— is impeded by deceit.

SPEAK TRUTH

Putting away lying, speak every man truth with
his neighbor: for we are members one of
another.

Christianity

Speak ye every man truth to his neighbor;
execute the judgment of truth and peace in your
gates.

Judaism

Him I call indeed a Brahmana who utters true
speech, instructive and free from harshness, so
that he offends no one

Buddhism

Do not clothe the truth with falsehood; do not knowingly conceal the truth.

Islam

Say what is true! Do thy duty. Do not swerve from the truth.

Hinduism

Sincerity is the way of Heaven, and to think how to be sincere is the way of a man. Never was there one possessed of complete sincerity who did not move others. Never was there one without sincerity who was able to move others.

Confucianism

MORE BLESSED TO GIVE
THAN TO RECEIVE

The wise handling of money can be as spir-
itually enriching as prayer. A person who
is in touch with his own inner self and who truly
loves his fellow man will experience his heart spontaneously overflowing with the desire to care for
others.

The giving of money, time, support, and en-
couragement to worthy causes can never be det-
rimental to the giver. The laws of nature are structured so that acts of charity will open an individual
to an unbounded reservoir of riches. Everything in
life has been created as the result of love and concern for others. When individuals give lovingly to
their brothers in the family of man, they establish
the basis for peace within every nation.

MORE BLESSED TO GIVE
THAN TO RECEIVE

It is more blessed to give than to receive.

Christianity

Extend your help without seeking reward. Give to others and do not regret or begrudge your liberality. Those who are thus are good.

Taoism

In the minds of the generous contentment is produced.

Sikhism

The poor, the orphan, the captive—feed them
for the love of God alone, desiring no reward,
nor even thanks.

Islam

Bounteous is he who gives to the beggar who
comes to him in want of food and feeble.

Hinduism

Blessed is he that considereth the poor: the Lord
will deliver him in time of trouble.

Judaism

21

HEAVEN IS
WITHIN

Life is structured so that the finest, most meaningful aspects are often hidden from outer exposure. The sweetness of an orange is hidden within a bitter skin. The seed of a tree, from which life will spring, is protected within a hard shell. And a man may walk the earth, not knowing that a vast depository of riches lies hidden deep within the ground beneath his feet.

From earliest childhood our senses respond to outward sensations. Without guidance and understanding, we could spend a lifetime appreciating the world only in an outward direction. But the true riches of life lie within. Through appreciation of the wisdom of the past, through prayer, and, most of all, through deep meditation, we can become one with the inner silence that is a part of God.

When that silence is reached, it begins to radiate throughout all of one's activities. When a large number of individuals radiate this inner silence, heaven will begin to be seen on earth.

HEAVEN IS WITHIN

The kingdom of God cometh not with
observation: neither shall they say, Lo here! or,
lo there! for, behold, the kingdom of God is
within you.

Christianity

What the undeveloped man seeks is outside;
what the advanced man seeks is within himself.

Confucianism

If you think the Law is outside yourself, you are
embracing not the absolute Law but some
inferior teaching.

Buddhism

Do not search in distant skies for God. In man's own heart is He found.

Shintoism

God bides hidden in the hearts of all.

Hinduism

Why wilt thou go into the jungles? What do you hope to find there? Even as the scent dwells within the flower, so God within thine own heart ever abides. Seek Him with earnestness and find Him there.

Sikhism

LOVE THY
NEIGHBOR

Every human being is born with an innate love for others. As a person matures, this love is put to many tests. Yet by understanding the teachings of the world's great religions, a person can find the faith he needs for his love to endure beyond life's hardships.

More than a passing glance at the scriptures is necessary to achieve this level of understanding. Acts of faith, prayer, and deep meditation provide us with the strength that allows love for our fellow man to become an abiding part of our lives, of our beings. When many of us attain this type of faith, the expression of love in the world will be as spontaneous and natural as love between mother and child.

LOVE THY NEIGHBOR

Thou shalt love thy neighbor as thyself.

Judaism

A new commandment I give to you, That you
love one another; even as I have loved you . . .
By this all men will know that you are my
disciples, if you have love for one another.

Christianity

A man obtains a proper rule of action by
looking on his neighbor as himself.

Hinduism

Full of love for all things in the world, practicing
virtue in order to benefit others, this man alone
is happy.

Buddhism

Seek to be in harmony with all your neighbors;
live in amity with your brethren.

Confucianism

Regard Heaven as your father, Earth as your
mother, and all things as your brothers and
sisters.

Shintoism

CONQUER
WITH LOVE

Whenever there is tension or fighting between individuals, groups, or nations, it
means that a time of mutual understanding has
been lost, and channels of communication have not
been used.

Love is a unifying force. It radiates outward to
resolve differences between people and nations. It
is not that these unique qualities dissolve and are
lost, but that they are integrated into a greater
whole in which they are made more useful and
beautiful.

Love conquers *before* there is fighting. Even if
channels of communication have broken down and
fighting breaks out, the underlying attitude should
still be one of love and unification by love.

CONQUER
WITH LOVE

Recompense evil, conquer it, with good.

Islam

Be not overcome of evil, but overcome evil
with good.

Christianity

With kindness conquer rage, with goodness
malice; with generosity defeat all meanness; with
the straight truth defeat lies and deceit.

Hinduism

A soft answer turns away wrath, but a harsh
word stirs up anger.

Judaism

Conquer your foe by force, and you increase his
anger. Conquer by love, and you will reap no
after-sorrow.

Buddhism

Love is sure to be victorious even in battle, and
firmly to maintain its ground. Heaven will save
its possessor, by his love protecting him.

Taoism

BLESSED ARE THE
PEACEMAKERS

When people live in the awareness that there is a close kinship between all individuals and nations, peace is the natural result. Peace can come about only as a result of concern and understanding for others. It can never be brought about by superficial negotiation or temporary agreement.

Peace certainly cannot be brought about by signatures on pieces of paper. Since the beginning of recorded history, tens of thousands of peace treaties have been signed between nations. Clearly, treaties cannot sustain peace. This is a lesson that must be learned finally and absolutely. It is time now to look toward deeper, more lasting feelings of love and understanding between people. This and this alone can bring sustained harmony in the world.

BLESSED ARE THE
PEACEMAKERS

Blessed are the peacemakers: for they shall be
called the children of God.

Christianity

Shall I tell you what acts are better than fasting,
charity, and prayers? Making peace between
enemies are such acts; for enmity and malice tear
up the heavenly rewards by the roots.

Islam

The noble minded dedicate themselves to the
promotion of peace and the happiness of
others—even those who injure them.

Hinduism

When righteousness is practiced to win peace, he
who so walks shall gain the victory and all
fetters utterly destroy.

Buddhism

How beautiful upon the mountains are the feet
of him who brings good tidings, who publishes
peace.

Judaism

AS YE SOW, SO
SHALL YE REAP

This is the great mystery of human life. This principle is so fundamental to each person's desires and goals that it forms a framework for activity throughout the day. For those who are aware that this principle is the determining factor in achieving happiness and success, the hours of the day become an attempt to act toward others with kindness and rightness. Those who are unaware struggle continously throughout their lives and do not know why. Aware or unaware, all are ruled by this inevitable law of nature.

AS YE SOW, SO SHALL YE REAP

It is nature's rule, that as we sow, we shall reap.

Buddhism

Whatever a man sows, that he will also reap.

Christianity

A liberal man will be enriched, and one who waters will himself be watered.

Judaism

What proceeds from you will return to you.

Confucianism

Thou canst not gather what thou dost not sow;
as thou dost plant the tree so it will grow.

Hinduism

Whatever man soweth, that shall he reap. If he
soweth trouble, trouble shall be his harvest. If a
man sow poison, he cannot expect ambrosia.

Sikhism

A MAN IS KNOWN BY HIS DEEDS, NOT BY HIS RELIGION

Inner life is the basis for outer activity. A person's actions are the mirror of his inner self. For this reason, when a man achieves an understanding of the spiritual aspects of human life, he spontaneously acts in a manner that encourages and supports a similar development of this knowledge in others. We need look no deeper than a man's outer activity to see the degree of his inner spiritual achievement.

A MAN IS KNOWN BY HIS DEEDS, NOT BY HIS RELIGION

God will not ask a man of what race he is. He will ask what he has done.

Sikhism

God will render to every man according to his deeds.

Christianity

A man asked Mohammad how to tell when one is truly faithful, and he replied: "If you derive pleasure from the good which you do and are grieved by the evil which you commit, then you are a true believer."

Islam

But I say unto you: deeds of love are worth as
much as all the commandments of the law.

Judaism

No brahmin is a brahmin by birth.
No outcaste is an outcaste by birth.
An outcaste is an outcaste by his deeds.
A brahmin is a brahmin by his deeds.

Buddhism

NOT WORDS OR
DETACHMENT, BUT ACTION

It is necessary, and perhaps one of our primary tasks on earth, to actively resolve the differences and disagreements between people.

Each person should have the goal to depart from this life having removed from the world all need for locks and keys and weapons and armor.

This goal may be too idealistic for many people—yet if no one on earth holds such an ideal, a state of peace and harmony will never reign on earth.

NOT WORDS OR
DETACHMENT, BUT ACTION

Not everyone that sayeth, Lord, Lord, shall
enter into the kingdom of heaven; but he that
doeth the will of my Father which is in heaven.

Christianity

Not learning but doing is the chief thing.

Judaism

Not in words does God get answers.

Taoism

Students and teachers, and all others,
Who read the mere words of ponderous books,
    know nothing,
But only waste their time in vain pursuit of
    words;
He who acts righteously is wise.

Hinduism

Like a beautiful flower, full of color, but
without scent, are the fine but fruitless words of
him who does not act accordingly.

Buddhism

BETTER TO
EXAMINE THE SELF

Our activities and successes are based on our inner strength and wholeness. To grow, it is necessary for us to recognize and correct our own faults. Yet it is difficult to do this since we hide our shortcomings not only from others but from ourselves.

When we gain the ability to recognize and correct our own bad habits, we begin to make rapid strides toward greater happiness and success in all spheres of life. Only by learning to admit to our own faults can we become more tolerant and loving to our fellow man and to his shortcomings.

BETTER TO
EXAMINE THE SELF

If you love others, and affection is not returned, look into your love. If you rule others, and they are unruly, look into your wisdom. If you treat others politely and they do not return your politeness, look into your respect. If your desires are not fulfilled, turn inward and examine yourself.

Confucianism

First take the log out of your own eye, and then you will see clearly to take the speck out of your brother's eye.

Christianity

The faults of others we see easily; our own are very difficult to see. Our neighbour's faults we winnow eagerly, as chaff from grain; our own we hide away as a cheat hides a losing roll of the dice.

Buddhism

He who knows others is discerning; he who knows himself is wise.

Taoism

They who quarrel with others, instead of quarreling with their own hearts, waste their lives.

Sikhism

BETTER TO RULE
THE SPIRIT

Through the ages, saints and sages of all religions have proclaimed that the human soul is unbounded and eternal. However different in outer expression, all religions have their source in this fundamental belief. Deep within each person is an individual consciousness that touches and is a part of the Universal Consciousness. Religion is that which allows this connection to be brought into our immediate awareness, and to be used practically in our day-to-day lives.

Since the length of an individual lifetime is brief compared to the infinity of time, it is wise to dedicate ourselves to the highest of goals.

BETTER TO RULE
THE SPIRIT

For what is a man profited, if he shall gain the
whole world, and lose his own soul?

Christianity

He who is slow to anger is better than the
mighty, and he who rules his spirit than he who
takes a city.

Judaism

If one were to conquer in battle a thousand times
a thousand men, he who conquers himself is the
greatest warrior.

Buddhism

He who restrains his rage from bolting
    with him,
He is true warrior and true charioteer,
Not he who slays in battle many foes.

Hinduism

He who overcomes others is strong; he who
overcomes himself is mighty.

Taoism

Difficult to conquer is one's self. But when that
is conquered, everything is conquered.

Jainism

57

WISDOM IS MORE
THAN RICHES

Wisdom is not a vague quality of mind. It is not a mood of resignation or detachment. Wisdom is a combination of experience and awareness that gives great dynamism to every activity undertaken. It is inner strength, intuitive creativity, and mental power. Wisdom allows a person to evaluate experiences of the past in a clear and orderly manner so that he can avoid further mistakes. It allows a person to look so deeply into present activities that glimpses of the future can be seen.

In the fullest sense, wisdom is a state of consciousness. Wisdom dawns when a person experiences the connection of his or her individual awareness with the Infinite. Then life is lived in the light of God, and all his undertakings are completely successful and fulfilling.

WISDOM IS MORE THAN RICHES

Riches are not from an abundance of worldly goods, but from a contented mind.

Islam

Lay not up for yourselves treasures upon earth, where moth and rust doth corrupt, and where thieves break through and steal. But lay up for yourselves treasures in heaven, where neither moth nor rust doth corrupt, and where thieves do not break through nor steal: for where your treasure is, there will your heart be also.

Christianity

The real treasure is that laid up by a man or
woman through charity and piety, temperance
and self control . . . The treasure thus hid is
secure, and does not pass away.

Buddhism

How much better is it to get wisdom than gold!
and to get understanding rather than silver!

Judaism

Knowledge is the best treasure that a man can
secretly hoard in life. Learning is the revered of
the revered. It is learning alone that enables a
man to better the conditions of his friends and
relations. Knowledge is the holiest of the holies,
the god of the gods, and commands respect of
crowned heads; shorn of it man is but an animal.

Hinduism

MAN DOES NOT LIVE
BY BREAD ALONE

The blessings of life are deeper than what can be appreciated by the senses. They are deeper even than what can be understood by the mind. Every aspect of life swirls with rhythms of the Divine. All activities, all successes, all well-being and happiness, have their basis in an unfathomable Spirit which sustains us even when we are not aware of it.

The fullest expression of the Divine is found in loving relationships between people. Life is nourished by kindness, by concern for others, by forgiving, by sharing, and by caring for all of God's creatures. Man does not live by material bread alone. He lives by a deeper power, one that creates and supports all the functions of life.

Man can express the fullness of the Divine. Every act of good, no matter how small, helps radiate the Divine throughout the world. The closer a person can come towards harmony with this power with this spirit of the Divine—the more joy life will have for him.

MAN DOES NOT LIVE
BY BREAD ALONE

Man shall not live by bread alone, but by every word of God.

Christianity

Man lives not by material bread alone.

Hinduism

Make divine knowledge thy food.

Sikhism

Man doth not live by bread only, but by every word that proceedeth out of the mouth of the Lord.

Judaism

The superior man deliberates upon how he may walk in truth, not upon what he may eat.

Confucianism

DO NOT HARM
ANYTHING

Just as we try to nourish and strengthen ourselves, so we should do the same for others. If someone tries to hurt another, it means that he is perceiving that person as something separate and foreign from himself.

We must remember that the feelings and hopes of others are the same as ours. Do not forget that all religions—which convey mankind's highest thoughts and aspirations—view all the people in the world as one great family.

DO NOT HARM
ANYTHING

Do not hurt others, do no one injury by thought
or deed, utter no word to pain thy fellow
creatures.

Hinduism

Hurt none by word or deed, be consistent in
well-doing.

Buddhism

Be ye kind to one another, tenderhearted,
forgiving one another, even as God for Christ's
sake hath forgiven you.

Christianity

Master of his senses and avoiding wrong, one
should do no harm to any living being, neither
by thoughts nor words nor acts.

Jainism

Whatever good you do for others, you send it
before your own soul and shall find it with God,
who sees all you do.

Islam

BLESSED TO
FORGIVE

How often does a mother forgive her infant? How often did Jesus forgive wrong? How often did Buddha, Mohammad, Shankara, and other enlightened teachers smile forgivingly at the faults of others?

We all will err at some point as we work through the lessons we must learn. Forgiveness is as necessary to life as the food we eat and the air we breathe. When an individual can cultivate an attitude of forgiveness, he helps to create a pocket of tranquillity in the world.

An attitude of forgiveness fosters channels of love and understanding in the heart. Years of education involving the study of books, laws and sayings cannot culture the intellect and emotions as can an attitude of forgiveness. Practicing forgiveness of others creates a habit that ultimately allows us to forgive events in our own past. Only then can life blossom into the fullness we desire.

BLESSED TO
FORGIVE

The most beautiful thing a man can do is to
forgive wrong.

Judaism

Then Peter came up and said to him, "Lord,
how often shall my brother sin against me, and I
forgive him? As many as seven times?" Jesus
said to him, "I do not say to you seven times,
but seventy times seven."

Christianity

Forgive thy servant seventy times a day.

Islam

Where there is forgiveness there is God himself.

Sikhism

Recompense injury with kindness.

Taoism

Never is hate diminished by hatred;
It is only diminished by love—
This is an eternal law.

Buddhism

BE SLOW
TO ANGER

Anger clouds the mind in the very moments that clarity and objectivity are needed most. Anger is the enemy of success and satisfaction. It rips apart the contented feeling in the mind. The more a person can stand apart and control sudden anger, the greater the chance for success in any undertaking, and the greater the chance for lasting fulfillment in life.

In the deepest sense, anger shows that a person feels he or she alone—not God—is responsible for the end result of an activity. Such a person can become very frustrated when obstacles suddenly arise. By remembering that there are many elements involved in success over which a person has little control, he can learn to diminish the fire of anger.

It has been said that when angry with loved ones, a person should count to ten before speaking. Actually, counting to ten is not long enough. Don't speak until calmness has been regained. If this takes an hour, or several hours, it is better than saying something that may be deeply regretted.

BE SLOW
TO ANGER

He who is slow to anger has great understanding, but he who has a hasty temper exalts folly.

Judaism

He who gives up anger attains to God.

Hinduism

Let not the sun go down upon your wrath.

Christianity

Let us cease from wrath and refrain from angry gestures.

Shintoism

He who holds back rising anger like a rolling chariot, him I call a real driver; others only hold the reins.

Buddhism

JUDGE NOT

Great philosophers have analyzed this principle for thousands of years, but for the person who is kind and thoughtful toward others, the meaning is simple and clear.

Like "As ye sow, so shall ye reap," and The Golden Rule, this principle is an expression of the underlying truth that mankind is one great family, and that we all spring from a common source.

JUDGE NOT

Judge not, and ye shall not be judged: condemn
not, and ye shall not be condemned: forgive, and
ye shall be forgiven.

Christianity

Judge not thy neighbor till thou art in his place.

Judaism

Judge not thy neighbor.

Buddhism

Follow that which is revealed to thee, and persevere with patience until God shall judge; for he is the best judge.

Islam

FOLLOW THE SPIRIT OF THE SCRIPTURES, NOT THE LETTER

Individual religions, like different nations and cultures, have unique characteristics. But these characteristics are only the surface aspects; the fundamental principles at the heart of all religions (like those at the core of all cultures and nations) are universal.

For this reason, the letters of the law, or the surface meanings found in the words of the teachings, are not as integral as the spirit of the law, which is universal and shared by all religions and cultures.

FOLLOW THE SPIRIT OF THE SCRIPTURES, NOT THE LETTER

The letter killeth, but the spirit giveth life.

Christianity

Rather let a letter be uprooted than the Torah be forgotten.

Judaism

The Koran was sent down in seven dialects, and in every one of its sentences there is an outer and an inner meaning.

Islam

Study the words, no doubt, but look
Behind them to the thought they indicate,
And having found it, throw the words away
As chaff when you have sifted out the grain.

Hinduism

Let not scholars scrutinize
The language of the wise too closely;
The seers think more of the thought
Than of the words in which 'tis caught.

Sufism

START WHEN YOUNG
TO SEEK WISDOM

When a seed germinates, it first sends a root downward into the earth. Only when the root is firmly established do limbs and branches begin to form. When constructing a skyscraper that will tower hundreds of feet in the air, builders first dig into the ground. Only when the foundation is complete does upward construction begin.

The same is true in a young person's growth. The stronger and more orderly the inner preparation, the greater the chance for fulfillment in life.

A great step is taken toward success and happiness when one becomes able to learn from the advice of others, not only from one's own successes and failures. Until that time, progress will be slow, and unnecessary suffering will result.

The most important advice to be understood and followed is the collected wisdom of the world's religions. This wisdom allows a person to establish an inner foundation for success and happiness. The younger a person is when he becomes aware of this, the easier it will be to accomplish all he wants in life.

START WHEN YOUNG
TO SEEK WISDOM

My son, gather instruction from thy youth up;
so shalt thou find wisdom till thine old age.

Judaism

Knowledge is riches, what one learns in youth is
engraven on stone.

Hinduism

Seek ye first the kingdom of God, and His
righteousness; and all these things shall be added
unto you.

Christianity

Seek knowledge from the cradle to the grave.

Islam

He who, even as a young student, applies
himself to the doctrine of truth, brightens up
this world like the moon set free from the
clouds.

Buddhism

BE WHOLEHEARTED

All success in life is the result of putting our attention into the proper channels and allowing a natural growth to occur. It is far too easy to let the mind remain divided, thinking about one thing or another, while trying to accomplish something important.

Working with a divided mind almost always gives results that are less than hoped for. But when a direct course is taken and a task is undertaken with dynamic, one-pointed perseverance, we can overcome even the most difficult obstacles.

Wheresoever you go, employ all your heart.

Confucianism

He who doubts is like a wave of the sea that is driven and tossed by the wind.

Christianity

Whatever your hand finds to do, do it with your might.

Judaism

Free yourself from doubt and you will find your
life quickened in the goodness of God.

Shintoism

Neither eating, nor fasting, nor penance, nor
sacrifice, nor observance of the seasons, purify a
mortal who has not conquered his doubt.

Buddhism

HONOR THE
ELDERLY

It is not in nature's plan for the elderly to be overly active in society, but they contribute in very important ways to the achievements of a nation. The gathered knowledge of the elderly in practical matters is immense. No person who has specific goals and aspirations should disregard the advice of these experienced individuals.

The more the aspirations of a society are based on the true nature of happiness—the lasting inner oneness with all things—the more a society will honor its aged members. Wisdom fills the elderly like water fills a reservoir. For this wellspring to flow, we must maintain a pipeline of respect.

HONOR THE
ELDERLY

He who always greets and constantly reveres the
aged, four things will increase to him: life,
beauty, happiness, power.

Buddhism

With the ancient is wisdom; and in length of
days understanding.

Judaism

Treat with reverence due to age the elders in
your own family.

Confucianism

Rebuke not an elder, but intreat him as a father.

Christianity

To honor an old man is to show respect for God.

Islam

OUR TRUE STRENGTH

Time exposes life's superficial aspects; only fundamental truths endure. When looking at ancient buildings, and monuments constructed thousands of years ago, we see that decorations and ornaments have vanished. Even walls and roofs have crumbled. Only foundations and central pillars remain. Similarly, the limbs and extremities of ancient statues often have fallen away, leaving only those portions supported by strong central structures.

The same is true in an individual's life. The ever-changing outer world gradually teaches a person to look for and appreciate inner, more lasting values. Ultimately each person is led to the realization that only his or her inner spirit remains untouched by change. The innermost nature of our Being remains steadfast through all passing joys and pains. It is at the core of our Being that our lives touch the Eternal, and it is from here that we derive our true strength.

OUR TRUE
STRENGTH

Deep within abides another life, not like the life of the senses, escaping sight, unchanging. This endures when all created things have passed away.

Hinduism

The peace of God, which passeth all understanding, shall keep your hearts and minds.

Christianity

God is our refuge and strength, a very present help in trouble. Therefore will not we fear, though the earth be removed, and though the mountains be carried into the midst of the sea.

Judaism

Be lamps unto yourselves. Be a refuge unto
yourselves. Seek not for refuge from anything
but the Self. Desires and tendencies pass away.
Only the Self abides.

Buddhism

Make honesty thy steed, truth thy saddle,
continence thine equestrian armor, the five
virtues thine arrows, and truth thy sword and
shield.

Sikhism

GOD IS
LOVE

In effect, this is the summation of all previous principles: God, the all-pervading oneness of spirit, is seen in essence as love.

The saints and sages of all religions have declared that they have drawn their wisdom from a universal source, and that this source is full of unbounded love and joy.

When believed and understood, the conviction that God is love will unite people everywhere.

GOD IS
LOVE

God is love, and he who abides in love abides in
God, and God abides in him.

Christianity

He that loveth not, knoweth not God. For God
is love.

Buddhism

Love is the beginning and end of the Torah.

Judaism

Love belongs to the high nobility of Heaven,
and is the quiet home where man should dwell.

Confucianism

Sane and insane, all are searching lovelorn
For Him, in mosque, temple, church, alike.
For only God is the One God of Love,
And Love calls from all these, each one
　　His home.

Sufism

MAN IS CREATED
IN GOD'S IMAGE

God is love, and man is made in God's image. How easy it is to be caught in the difficulties of life and forget the basic underlying truths that are simple and straightforward.

Even in the midst of our busy world there are saints and sages working ceaselessly to infuse these simple truths into our complex lives. These noble souls radiate the divinity that is the inner basis of man's existence.

Regular periods of meditation and prayer will center us in the awareness of the underlying truths, so that we can recognize the divine within ourselves and radiate this understanding to others around us.

MAN IS CREATED
IN GOD'S IMAGE

God created man in His own image, in the
image of God created He him.

Judaism

The individual soul is nothing else in essence
than universal soul.

Hinduism

On God's own nature has been molded man's.

Islam

God is concealed in every heart; his light is in
every heart.

Sikhism

Know ye not that ye are the temple of God, and
that the Spirit of God dwelleth in you?

Christianity

LIVING IN
UNITY

Fostering growth and development is as natural to a society as desiring advancement in life is to an individual. The greater the harmony and peace in a nation, the greater is the opportunity for firmly established financial, spiritual, and educational organizations to develop. These organizations allow individuals and the society as a whole to progress.

The joy of living in society is that each person can derive benefits from every other person's efforts. Each person contributes a little, and then receives the vast benefit of society's achievements.

Material needs and comforts are only one aspect of this collective benefit; a greater aspect is the collective wisdom of the spiritual truths that are passed from generation to generation. This wisdom serves as a practical basis for achieving fulfillment in life.

LIVING IN
UNITY

God hath made of one blood all nations of men.
Christianity

Behold, how good and pleasant it is when
brothers dwell in unity!
Judaism

All creatures are the family of God; and he is the
most beloved of God who does most good unto
His family.
Islam

Human beings all are as head, arms, trunk, and legs unto one another.

Hinduism

Do not forget that the world is one great family.

Shintoism

113

PRAYERS OF THE RELIGIONS

The prayers of the world's religions have a common theme: the desire and need to make contact with God, and to be shown by Him the path on earth that leads to freedom, health, prosperity, and knowledge.

At its core, religion is extremely practical; its purpose is to lead mankind to greater happiness, achievement, and inner peace. These are the things that every person wants. These aspirations are the goals of life.

The central prayers of the religions ask for guidance in achieving these aspirations. Their common goal shows the essential oneness of the human spirit.

PRAYERS OF THE RELIGIONS

Our Father who art in heaven, Hallowed be thy name. Thy kingdom come, Thy will be done, On earth as it is in heaven. Give us this day our daily bread; And forgive us our debts, As we also have forgiven our debtors; And lead us not into temptation, But deliver us from evil. Amen.

Christianity

Lead me, O Lord, in Thy righteousness. Make Thy way straight before me. Cleanse Thou me from hidden faults. Keep back Thy servant from presumptuous sins; let my sins not have dominion over me . . . Show me Thy ways, O Lord. Teach me Thy paths, and lead me in Thy truth. Thou art the God of my salvation.

Judaism

Praise be to God, the Lord of all creatures; the most merciful, the king of the day of judgment. Thee do we worship, and of thee do we beg assistance. Direct us in the right way, in the way of those to whom thou hast been gracious; not of those against whom thou art incensed, nor of those who go astray.

Islam

Supreme Lord! Lord of warmth and light,
Of life and consciousness, that knows all,
Guide us by the right path to happiness,
And give us strength and will to war against
The sins that rage in us and lead us astray.
We bow in reverence and prayer to Thee. Aum.

Hinduism

Aum! Amīn! Āmēn! Amen!

SOURCES

Ballou, Robert O., ed. *The Bible of the World*. New York: The Viking Press, 1939.

Champion, Selwyn Gurney, and Short, Dorothy. *Readings from World Religions*. Boston: The Beacon Press, 1951.

Das, Bhagavan. *The Essential Unity of All Religions*. Wheaton, Ill.: The Theosophical Press, 1939.

Frost, S.E. Jr., ed. *The Sacred Writings of the World's Greatest Religions*. New York: McGraw-Hill, 1943.

Gaer, Joseph. *The Wisdom of the Living Religions*. New York: Dodd, Mead & Company, 1956.

The Holy Bible. King James Version.

The Holy Bible. Revised Standard Version.

The Koran. Trans. George Sale. Philadelphia: J.B. Lippincott & Co., 1864.

Legge, James, D.D., L.L.D. *The Life and Works of Mencius*. London: Trübner and Co., 1875.

Macauliffe, Max Arthur. *The Sikh Religion: Its Gurus, Sacred Writings and Authors*. Vol. 1. Bombay, India: Oxford University Press, 1963.

Oriental Literature: The Literature of China (Including the Analects of Confucius). Rev. ed. New York: The Colonial Press, 1900.

The Sacred Books of China: The Texts of Taoism. Trans. James Legge. London: Oxford University Press, 1891.

Sacred Books of the East (Including the Vedic Hymns and The Dhammapada of Buddhism). Rev. ed. New York: P.F. Collier & Sons, 1900.

119

ABOUT THE AUTHOR

JEFFREY MOSES has an M.A. in the philosophy of
education from the University of Colorado. A freelance
writer and advertising executive, Moses has spent the
last ten years researching the world's great scriptures.
He has traveled across the country lecturing to college
and business people on the benefits of meditation and
stress reduction techniques.

Jeffrey Moses lives with his wife, Ruth, in Kansas
City, Missouri.